Little Pebble™

What Are Droughts?

by Mari Schuh

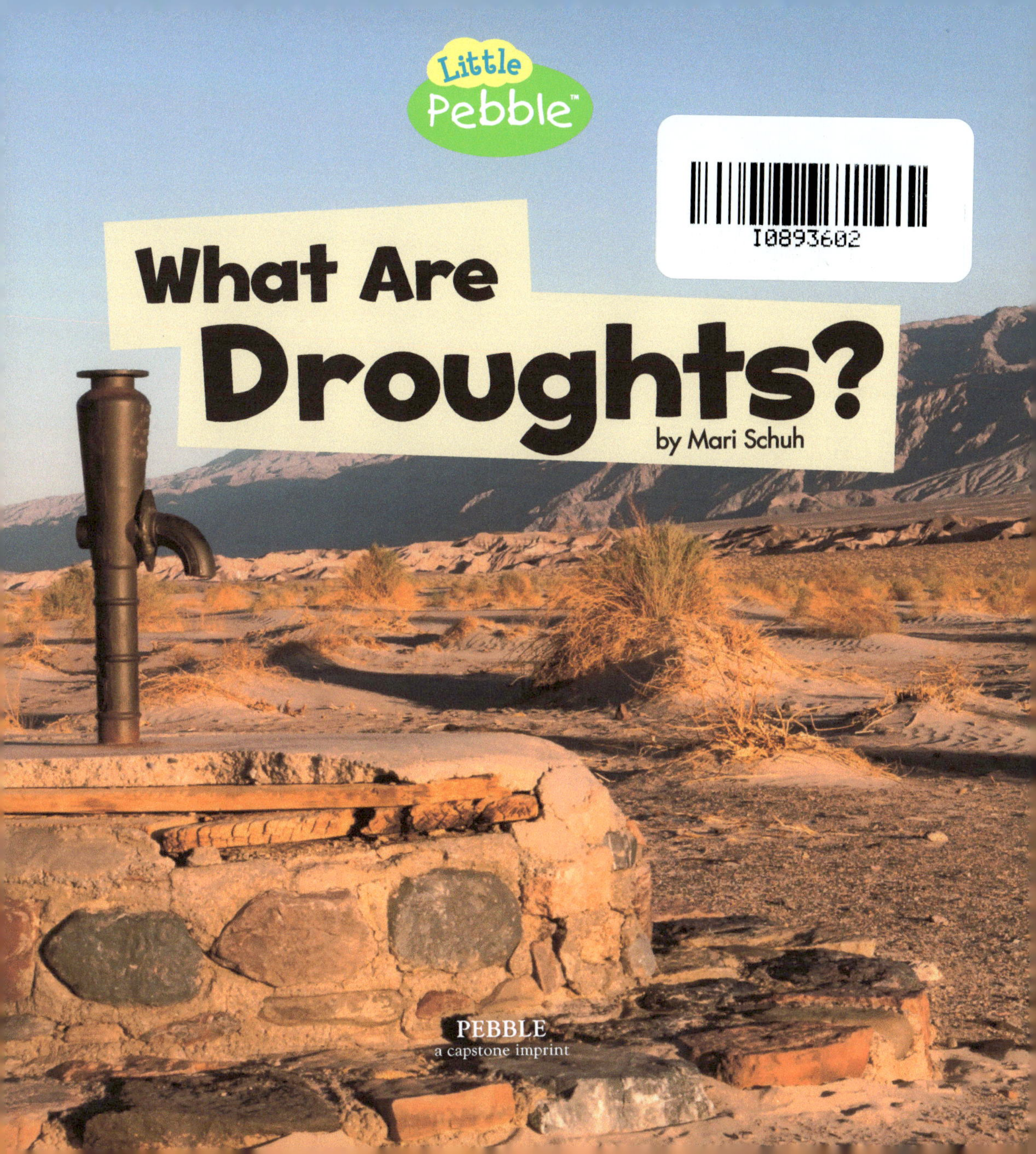

PEBBLE
a capstone imprint

Little Pebble is published by Pebble
1710 Roe Crest Drive,
North Mankato, Minnesota 56003
www.mycapstone.com

Library of Congress Cataloging-in-Publication Data
Names: Schuh, Mari C., 1975–author.
Title: What are droughts? / by Mari Schuh.
Description: North Mankato, Minnesota : Pebble, a Capstone imprint, [2019] | Series: Little pebble. Wicked weather | Audience: Ages 4–8.
Identifiers: LCCN 2018029835 (print) | LCCN 2018031583 (ebook) | ISBN 9781977103390 (eBook PDF) | ISBN 9781977103321 (hardcover) | ISBN 9781977105493 (paperback)
Subjects: LCSH: Droughts—Juvenile literature.
Classification: LCC QC929.25 (ebook) | LCC QC929.25 .S38 2019 (print) | DDC 551.57/73—dc23
LC record available at https://lccn.loc.gov/2018029835

Editorial Credits
Nikki Potts, editor; Kyle Grenz, designer;
Heather Mauldin, media researcher; Tori Abraham, production specialist

Photo Credits
Alamy: Jesper Jensen, 19; iStockphoto: cinoby, 5, DougVonGausig, 17, ksteffens, 11, Marccophoto, 9; Shutterstock: A Luna Blue, 21, Christopher Boswell, 1, Galyna Andrushko, cover, orin, 7, Sundry Photography, 15, Tero Vesalainen, 13

Printed in the United States 5188

Table of Contents

What Is a Drought?

The ground is dry.

Little rain falls.

A drought has begun.

A drought happens slowly.

It can last for years.

Fields are dry.

Crops cannot grow.

There is less food to eat.

Lakes and rivers dry up.

Fish may die.

Saving and Finding Water

People use less water.

They take shorter showers.

Way to go!

What is that?

It is a lake.

It is called a reservoir.

reservoir

These lakes hold water. People can use the water when it is dry.

Look!

People dig a well.

They find water.

It is deep in the ground.

It Rains

See the clouds.

Rain!

The drought is ending!

It rains again and again.

Glossary

crop—a plant farmers grow in large amounts, usually for food; farmers grow crops such as corn, soybeans, and peas

drought—a long period of weather with little or no rainfall

field—an area of land used for growing crops

reservoir—a huge lake that has been made to store water

well—a deep hole from which people can draw water

Read More

Meister, Cari. *Droughts.* Disaster Zone. Minneapolis: Pogo Books, 2016.

Rivera, Andrea. *Droughts.* Zoom in on Natural Disasters. Minneapolis: Abdo Zoom, 2018.

Rustad, Martha E. H. *Droughts: Be Aware and Prepare.* Weather Aware. North Mankato, Minn.: Capstone Press, 2015.

Internet Sites

Use FactHound to find Internet sites related to this book.

Visit www.facthound.com

Just type in 9781977103321 and go.

Critical Thinking Questions

1. How do droughts hurt people, crops, and animals?
2. Name one way people can save water.
3. How long can a drought last?

Index